STUDY GUIDE

THE ENDURANCE FACTOR

Copyright © 2023 by Greg Surratt and Chip Judd

Published by AVAIL

All rights reserved. No portion of this book may be reproduced, stored in a retrieval system, or transmitted in any form or by any means—electronic, mechanical, photocopy, recording, scanning, or other—except for brief quotations in critical reviews or articles, without prior written permission of the author.

Unless otherwise specified, Scripture quotations are taken from the (NASB®) New American Standard Bible®, Copyright © 1960, 1971, 1977, 1995, 2020 by The Lockman Foundation. Used by permission. All rights reserved. www.lockman.org | Scripture quotations marked NIV are taken from the Holy Bible, New International Version®, NIV®. Copyright © 1973, 1978, 1984, 2011 by Biblica, Inc.™ Used by permission of Zondervan. All rights reserved worldwide. www.zondervan.com. The "NIV" and "New International Version" are trademarks registered in the United States Patent and Trademark Office by Biblica, Inc.™ | Scripture quotations marked NLT are taken from the Holy Bible, New Living Translation, copyright © 1996, 2004, 2015 by Tyndale House Foundation. Used by permission of Tyndale House Publishers, Inc., Carol Stream, Illinois 60188. All rights reserved.

For foreign and subsidiary rights, contact the author.

Cover design by: Sara Young
Cover photo by: Kim Graham

ISBN: 978-1-959095-76-7   1 2 3 4 5 6 7 8 9 10

Printed in the United States of America

STUDY GUIDE

THE ENDURANCE FACTOR

GREG SURRATT AND CHIP JUDD

CONTENTS

CHAPTER 1. **The Day My World Turned Upside Down** 6

CHAPTER 2. **We're All Frogs** 12

CHAPTER 3. **A Price Too High** 18

CHAPTER 4. **The Long Road Down** 24

CHAPTER 5. **Lookin' for Love** 30

CHAPTER 6. **The Long Road Back** 36

CHAPTER 7. **Building Resilient Teams** 44

CHAPTER 8. **It's (Almost) Never Too Late** 50

THE ENDURANCE FACTOR

How ministry leaders can avoid burnout, live well, and finish strong

GREG SURRATT AND CHIP JUDD

CHAPTER I

THE DAY MY WORLD TURNED UPSIDE DOWN

If you commit yourself to living well, you will exponentially multiply the chances that you will finish strong.

READING TIME

As you read Chapter 1: "The Day My World Turned Upside Down" in *The Endurance Factor*, review, reflect on, and respond to the text by answering the following questions.

REFLECT AND TAKE ACTION:

What does finishing strong mean to you? What leaders do you know who have finished strong?

_____
_____
_____
_____
_____
_____
_____
_____
_____
_____

What are some factors that prohibit people from finishing strong?

_____
_____
_____
_____
_____
_____
_____
_____
_____
_____

How stressed are you in your current position on a scale of 1-10? Has this stress increased or decreased recently?

1   2   3   4   5   6   7   8   9   10

_____
_____
_____
_____
_____
_____

Who do you have in your life that you can go to in total honesty?

_____
_____
_____
_____
_____
_____

Who do you have that can comfort and energize you when you need it most? Are you this person for someone else as well?

_____
_____
_____
_____
_____
_____

> *For our struggle is not against flesh and blood, but against the rulers, against the powers, against the world forces of this darkness, against the spiritual forces of wickedness in the heavenly places.*
>
> *—Ephesians 6:12*

Consider the scripture above and answer the following questions:

How should this verse affect our perspective and how we treat others?

_____
_____
_____
_____
_____
_____
_____
_____

Can you live the way you're living right now for decades? If not, what needs to change?

_____
_____
_____
_____
_____
_____
_____

Are you on target to accomplish your vision? Why or why not?

_____
_____
_____
_____
_____
_____
_____
_____
_____
_____

If you keep living the way you're living right now, what will your relationship with God look like in five, ten, or fifteen years? Will you be closer to Him, or farther away?

_____
_____
_____
_____
_____
_____
_____
_____
_____
_____
_____

When was the last time you felt stuck in an area of your life? Who did you turn to for help? Why do you feel stuck in this area?

_____
_____
_____
_____
_____
_____
_____
_____
_____

What internal barriers in your thoughts, beliefs, or behaviors do you need to overcome in order to embrace the future God has for you?

_____
_____
_____
_____
_____
_____
_____
_____
_____

CHAPTER 2

WE'RE ALL FROGS

Real freedom awaits us if we're willing to take off our masks and experience the depth of relationship that God designed us for.

READING TIME

As you read Chapter 2: "We're All Frogs" in *The Endurance Factor*, review, reflect on, and respond to the text by answering the following questions.

REFLECT AND TAKE ACTION:

What is your identity? What is your identity, worth, and value rooted in?

_____
_____
_____
_____
_____
_____
_____
_____
_____
_____

Why is it important to understand that we're both deeply flawed and dearly loved? What happens when each of those is minimized?

_____
_____
_____
_____
_____
_____
_____
_____
_____
_____

What is your calling? Has this calling changed over the years?

_____
_____
_____
_____
_____
_____
_____
_____
_____
_____
_____
_____

What is your assignment? How does this differ from your calling?

_____
_____
_____
_____
_____
_____
_____
_____
_____
_____
_____
_____

> "Can a woman forget her nursing child
> And have no compassion on the son of her womb?
> Even these may forget, but I will not forget you.
> Behold, I have inscribed you on the palms of My hands;
> Your walls are continually before Me. . . ."
> —Isaiah 49:15-16

Consider the scripture above and answer the following questions:

In your own words, what is the meaning of this verse?

_____
_____
_____
_____
_____
_____
_____
_____
_____

How do you think this verse should affect how we live and what we do?

_____
_____
_____
_____
_____
_____
_____

Have you ever fallen into the cycle of comparison? What was the outcome? How do you defend against it now?

_____
_____
_____
_____
_____
_____
_____
_____
_____

Have you ever witnessed someone burnout? Were there warning signs?

_____
_____
_____
_____
_____
_____
_____
_____
_____
_____
_____

Do you manage your emotions in a healthy way? What aspect of your emotional life do you need to work on?

What are spiritual rhythms? What are some of your spiritual rhythms?

CHAPTER 3

A PRICE TOO HIGH

An organization's culture is a reflection of its leader. No one else has the power and the microphone the leader possesses.

READING TIME

As you read Chapter 3: "A Price Too High" in *The Endurance Factor*, review, reflect on, and respond to the text by answering the following questions.

REFLECT AND TAKE ACTION:

Do you agree that our #1 purpose is to be loved by God? What difference would it make in your life if you regularly received and rested in God's love for you? How would it change The Church if God's love became the source of our identity, affection, and approval?

_____
_____
_____
_____
_____
_____
_____
_____
_____

Read Ephesians 2:1-10 and make observations about the transformation of our identity.

_____
_____
_____
_____
_____
_____
_____
_____

Has your organization ever gotten so caught up in increasing church metrics that they lose sight of the real mission? Explain.

_____
_____
_____
_____
_____
_____
_____
_____
_____
_____

> "Has a nation changed gods,
> When they were not gods?
> But My people have exchanged their glory
> For that which is of no benefit.
> Be appalled at this, you heavens,
> And shudder, be very desolate," declares the LORD.
>
> —Jeremiah 2:11-12

Consider the scripture above and answer the following questions:

What stands out to you from this verse?

_____
_____
_____
_____
_____

Do you think some pastors, leaders, and churches idolize church metrics? Explain your answer.

As a church, who or what is your primary responsibility to?

At what point does wanting to grow your church become negative?

How do you define success in your church? Has this changed over the years?

_____
_____
_____
_____
_____
_____
_____
_____
_____
_____
_____
_____

What has God been saying to you through this chapter? What's your next step?

_____
_____
_____
_____
_____
_____
_____
_____
_____

CHAPTER 4

THE LONG ROAD DOWN

The greatest obstacles between you and the future you want are inside of you, not outside.

READING TIME

As you read Chapter 4: "The Long Road Down" in *The Endurance Factor*, review, reflect on, and respond to the text by answering the following questions.

REFLECT AND TAKE ACTION:

Review the stages of burnout in the beginning of this chapter. What is the farthest down that progression that you have ever gone? What factors contributed to this slide? What brought you back? Where are you now?

What are some reasons it's so easy to deny, minimize, and rationalize every step toward utter collapse?

_____
_____
_____
_____
_____
_____
_____
_____
_____

What stands out to you from the story of Elijah and the drought told in this chapter?

_____
_____
_____
_____
_____
_____
_____
_____
_____
_____
_____
_____

What type of "lens" (or perspective) was Elijah looking through?

___

Take some time to reflect on your childhood. How do you think your life has been affected by genetic predisposition, imprinting, and your life choices?

___

What's one area of your life you want God to work on? How do you want Him to change you in this area?

_____
_____
_____
_____
_____
_____
_____
_____
_____
_____
_____
_____

Do you feel you have both security and significance? Where do these come from?

_____
_____
_____
_____
_____
_____
_____
_____
_____
_____
_____

What is God saying to you through this chapter?

_____
_____
_____
_____
_____
_____
_____
_____
_____
_____
_____
_____
_____
_____

CHAPTER 5

LOOKIN' FOR LOVE

It's perfectly fine for people to appreciate us and our messages, but we cross a line when we have to have it to feel okay about ourselves.

READING TIME

As you read Chapter 5: "Lookin' for Love" in *The Endurance Factor*, review, reflect on, and respond to the text by answering the following questions.

REFLECT AND TAKE ACTION:

Has your desire for attention or affirmation from the crowd ever distracted you from your message? Explain.

_____
_____
_____
_____
_____
_____
_____
_____
_____
_____

What's important to you? To what source do you turn to get your deepest needs met?

_____
_____
_____
_____
_____
_____
_____
_____
_____
_____

Read Psalm 73. How did comparison affect the writer? What got him out of his funk? Can you see yourself in this psalm? Explain your answer.

___

Have you tried to fill the hole that only God's love can fill with something or someone else? What was it? What was the outcome?

___

> *"If you love Me, you will keep My commandments."*
> —John 14:15

Consider the scripture above and answer the following questions:

What is the significance of "If you love me" coming first in this verse?

_____
_____
_____
_____
_____
_____
_____
_____
_____

How do we combat comparison and idolatry?

_____
_____
_____
_____
_____
_____
_____
_____

Where do you draw the line between listening to those around you and living for those around you?

___

What other needs do you have? Have you ever tried to fulfill these needs somewhere ineffective? Explain.

___

CHAPTER 6

THE LONG ROAD BACK

The deeper change happens in us, the wider our impact on the people around us.

READING TIME

As you read Chapter 6: "The Long Road Back" in *The Endurance Factor*, review, reflect on, and respond to the text by answering the following questions.

REFLECT AND TAKE ACTION:

How often do you look back and recognize how far God has brought you? Why don't you realize where He is taking you in the moment?

_____
_____
_____
_____
_____
_____
_____
_____
_____

What stands out to you from the testimonials following the retreats? Do you think you and your team could benefit from this type of retreat?

_____
_____
_____
_____
_____
_____
_____
_____

What can you do for your team that blends grace, truth, and time?

___

> *Therefore be imitators of God, as beloved children; and walk in love, just as Christ also loved you and gave Himself up for us, an offering and sacrifice to God as a fragrant aroma.*
>
> —Ephesians 5:1-2

Consider the scripture above and answer the following questions:

Do you "walk in love"? How? Explain your answer.

___

How can we imitate God in everything we do? What does this look like?

How have you changed as a person throughout your life journey? Are you willing to change more?

How can we know what we need to change within ourselves in order to move into the future God has planned out for us?

_____
_____
_____
_____
_____
_____
_____
_____
_____
_____

Which of the four habits discussed (find your band of brothers or sisters, develop a conversational relationship with God through journaling, learn to go to God first and most for everything you need, detox your soul by killing your ANTs) do you most need to work on? Why?

_____
_____
_____
_____
_____
_____
_____
_____

Which of the four habits above do you feel you are already proficient at, if any? Explain your answer.

Think of the last ANT you had—and yes, you had one! Use the three-part strategy to combat your ANT:

» Capture:

» Question:

» Replace:

What are the triggers (recurring events or people) that produce ANTs instantly in your mind and heart? How would making this process—capture, question, and replace—an embodied habit help you?

CHAPTER 7

BUILDING RESILIENT TEAMS

The key to creating a healthy team, a healthy church, and a healthy family is to pursue your own health. There's no shortcut, and there's no alternative.

READING TIME

As you read Chapter 7: "Building Resilient Teams" in *The Endurance Factor*, review, reflect on, and respond to the text by answering the following questions.

REFLECT AND TAKE ACTION:

How would you rate your team's current resiliency level on a scale from 1-10?

1   2   3   4   5   6   7   8   9   10

_____
_____
_____

In your own words, how would you define resiliency?

_____
_____
_____
_____
_____
_____

Does your organizational culture support your vision? In what ways? In what ways could it better support your vision?

_____
_____
_____
_____
_____
_____
_____
_____
_____

THE ENDURANCE FACTOR: STUDY GUIDE | 45

> And He said to him, "YOU SHALL LOVE THE LORD YOUR GOD WITH ALL YOUR HEART, AND WITH ALL YOUR SOUL, AND WITH ALL YOUR MIND." This is the great and foremost commandment.
>
> —Matthew 22:37-38

Consider the scripture above and answer the following questions:

Is this verse represented in any way within your organizational culture? Where?

_____
_____
_____
_____
_____
_____
_____
_____
_____
_____

What are some of the benefits of a positive and healthy organizational culture?

_____
_____
_____
_____
_____

What cultural responsibilities does your organization have? How do they differ from the four cultural responsibilities provided in this chapter?

Take some time to list your wants and needs (and be ruthlessly honest):

» In my life and ministry, I want:

» To feel good about myself, I need:

_____
_____
_____
_____
_____

How do you invest in others? How do you think this affects the organization's culture?

_____
_____
_____
_____
_____
_____
_____
_____
_____

How often do you go out of your way to disciple leaders? How do you do this?

_____
_____
_____
_____
_____

Other than your words, how do you positively influence others and your organizational culture?

Think back over your interactions with your team over the past week, and ask yourself: Can I picture Jesus saying what I said and doing what I did the way I said and did it?

CHAPTER 8

IT'S (ALMOST) NEVER TOO LATE

Don't waste your pain! The best way to avoid wasting pain is to learn from it.

READING TIME

As you read Chapter 8: "It's (Almost) Never Too Late" in *The Endurance Factor*, review, reflect on, and respond to the text by answering the following questions.

REFLECT AND TAKE ACTION:

Take time to reassess your assignment. What is your responsibility? How do you get it done?

_____
_____
_____
_____
_____
_____
_____

How has your responsibility changed? Is there any segment of your responsibilities you actually should not be worrying about?

_____
_____
_____
_____
_____
_____
_____
_____
_____
_____
_____

THE ENDURANCE FACTOR: STUDY GUIDE | 51

Read Galatians 6:9. How does Paul address our discouragement and exhaustion? What would he say to you right now?

___

> *For our momentary, light affliction is producing for us an eternal weight of glory far beyond all comparison, while we look not at the things which are seen, but at the things which are not seen for the things which are seen are temporal, but the things which are not seen are eternal.*
> —2 Corinthians 4:17-18

Consider the scripture above and answer the following questions:

What is the meaning of this verse?

___

Does this verse encourage you in the painful moments of your journey? How?

___

How is God pruning you in your life? What changes does He want you to make?

___

What do you see when you look in the mirror of your most important relationships?

___

As you close this book and move forward in your life and leadership, what are some of the major changes you are going to make?

_____
_____
_____
_____
_____
_____
_____
_____
_____

What unhealthy or ineffective habits, perspectives, and practices are you going to leave behind?

_____
_____
_____
_____
_____
_____
_____
_____
_____

Printed in the USA
CPSIA information can be obtained
at www.ICGtesting.com
LVHW051242121023
760674LV00069B/1726